Welcome
to the World,

ZooBorns!

by Andrew Bleiman and Chris Eastland

The photos in this book were previously published in
ZooBorns: The Newest, Cutest Animals from the World's Zoos and Aquariums.

Ready-to-Read

Simon Spotlight
New York   London   Toronto   Sydney   New Delhi

SIMON SPOTLIGHT

An imprint of Simon & Schuster Children's Publishing Division

1230 Avenue of the Americas, New York, New York 10020

Text copyright © 2012 by ZooBorns LLC

Photos copyright © 2010 by ZooBorns LLC

The photos in this book were previously published in *ZooBorns: The Newest, Cutest Animals from the World's Zoos and Aquariums*. All rights reserved, including the right of reproduction in whole or in part in any form. SIMON SPOTLIGHT, READY-TO-READ, and colophon are registered trademarks of Simon & Schuster, Inc. For information about special discounts for bulk purchases, please contact Simon & Schuster Special Sales at 1-866-506-1949 or business@simonandschuster.com.

Manufactured in China 0915 SDI

Welcome to the wonderful world of
ZooBorns!

The newborn animals featured in this book live
in zoos around the world. Get to know them through
adorable photos and fun facts written in language that is
just right for emerging readers. Your child might not be
able to pronounce all the animal species names yet, but if
you stay close by, you can help sound them out.

This book can also be used as a tool to begin a
conversation about endangered species. The more
we learn about animals in zoos, the more we can do
to protect animals in the wild. Please visit your
local accredited zoo or aquarium to learn more!

This is Amani the aardvark.
Amani has such big ears
and so many wrinkles!

Welcome to the world,
baby aardvark!

Here is a newborn clouded leopard.
This little kitten will grow into a big cat.
Look at his milk mustache!

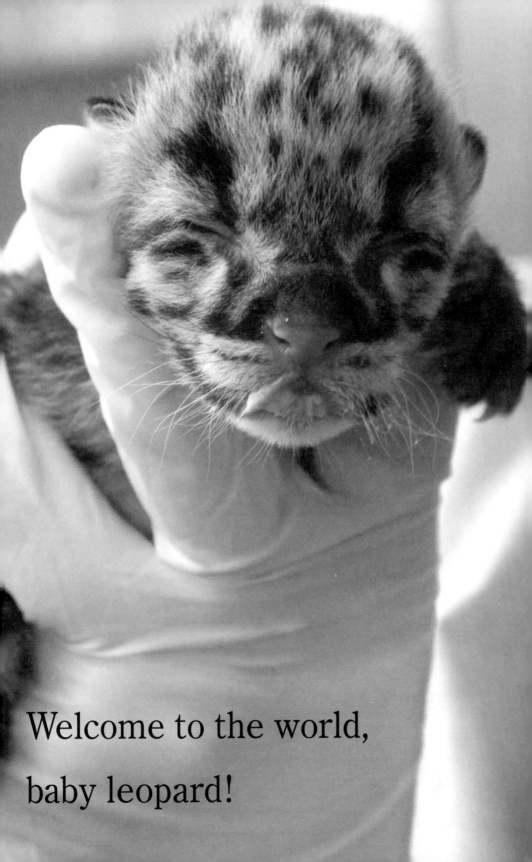

Welcome to the world,
baby leopard!

Say hello to Lana and Lucy!
Lana and Lucy are twin
emperor tamarins.

Welcome to the world,
baby tamarins!

One, two, three
baby meerkats
are hiding in a burrow.
Soon they will come out to
explore.

Welcome to the world,
baby meerkats!

Splish, splash!

Kit the sea otter is a great swimmer.

Kit swims with a shell in her paws.

Welcome to the world,
baby sea otter!

Meet Kali and Durga.
They are brother and sister
Bengal tigers.
They have blue eyes
and white fur.

Welcome to the world,
baby tigers!

Mali the elephant loves to smile!
She also loves to have fun.
Her trunk will grow to be long and strong.

Welcome to the world, baby elephant!

One fact about
Oliver the koala
is that he is not a bear!
Another fact about Oliver
is that he loves his mommy!

Welcome to the world,
baby koala!

Kai the spotted hyena
likes to sleep
with his legs in the air.
That is so silly!

Welcome to the world,
baby hyena!

These baby mongooses
rest all together
in a big, furry heap!
Welcome to the world,
baby mongooses!

Special thanks to the photographers and institutions that made ZooBorns! possible:

AARDVARK
Amani
Mark M. Gaskill, Phoenix Innovate,
taken at the Detroit Zoo

TIGERS
Kali and Durga
Robert La Follette, taken at Tampa's Lowry Park

TAMARINS
Lana and Lucy
Dave Parsons/Denver Zoo

ELEPHANT
Mali
Trent Browning/Melbourne Zoo

MEERKATS
Zoo Basel

CLOUDED LEOPARD
Smithsonian National Zoological Park

KOALA
Oliver
Richard Rokes/Riverbanks Zoo and Garden

SEA OTTER
Kit
Randy Wilder/© Monterey Bay Aquarium

HYENA
Kai
Dave Parsons/Denver Zoo

BANDED MONGOOSES
Cheryl Piropato/Fort Wayne Children's Zoo

I Love You,

ZooBorns!

by Andrew Bleiman and Chris Eastland

Most of the photos in this book were previously published in
ZooBorns: The Newest, Cutest Animals from the World's Zoos and Aquariums.

Ready-to-Read

Simon Spotlight
New York   London   Toronto   Sydney   New Delhi

SIMON SPOTLIGHT
An imprint of Simon & Schuster Children's Publishing Division
1230 Avenue of the Americas, New York, New York 10020
Text copyright © 2012 by ZooBorns LLC
Photos copyright © 2010, 2012 by ZooBorns LLC
Most of the photos in this book were previously published in *ZooBorns: The Newest, Cutest Animals from the World's Zoos and Aquariums*. All rights reserved, including the right of reproduction in whole or in part in any form.
SIMON SPOTLIGHT, READY-TO-READ, and colophon are registered trademarks of Simon & Schuster, Inc.
For information about special discounts for bulk purchases, please contact Simon & Schuster Special Sales at
1-866-506-1949 or business@simonandschuster.com.
Manufactured in China 0915 SDI

Welcome to the wonderful world of
ZooBorns!

The newborn animals featured in this book live
in zoos around the world. Get to know them through
adorable photos and fun facts written in language that is
just right for emerging readers. Your child might not be
able to pronounce all the animal species names yet, but if
you stay close by, you can help sound them out.

This book can also be used as a tool to begin a
conversation about endangered species. The more
we learn about animals in zoos, the more we can do
to protect animals in the wild. Please visit your
local accredited zoo or aquarium to learn more!

Good morning!
This giant panda is ready
to start his day.

I love you, baby panda!

It is bath time for
Prince Harry, the baby
pygmy hippo.
He loves to splash
in the water.

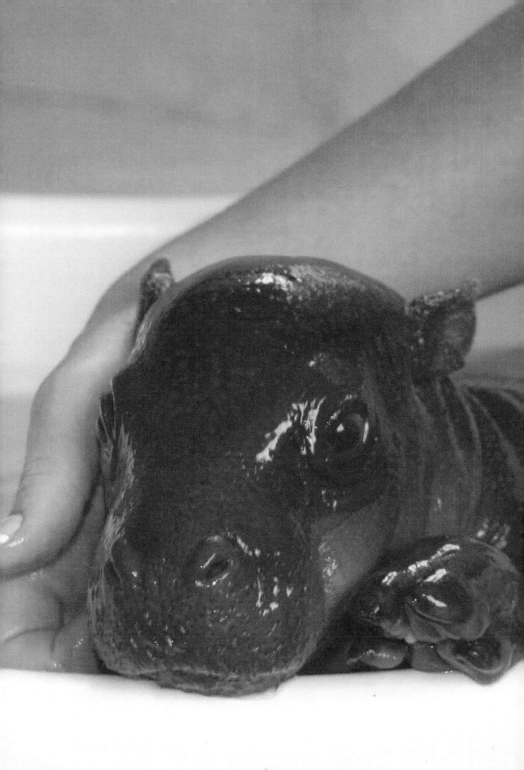

I love you, baby hippo!

Sawyer is a tawny frogmouth.
This bird loves to hop from one foot to the other.

I love you, baby frogmouth!

This common wombat loves lunchtime!
But he sleeps during the day, so he eats lunch in the middle of the night.

I love you, baby wombat!

What do the baby
wildcats see?
They are all
very curious kitties!

I love you, baby wildcats!

Penguins love to waddle from place to place. They also love to slide across the ice to get to where they are going. This baby gentoo penguin is ready to slide.

I love you, baby penguin!

Lucy, the emperor tamarin, loves being brushed. She is so small that the zookeeper uses a toothbrush!

I love you, baby tamarin!

When these otter pups are
awake, they are very noisy.
They love to chirp.

Right now, they are snuggling in a big pile.

I love you, baby otters!

Tahina, the crowned
sifaka lemur, is very tiny.

She loves to hug
her big stuffed teddy bear.
I love you, baby lemur!

Rooby, the red kangaroo, loves being wrapped up in a warm blanket. It feels just like she is in her mom's pouch!

I love you, baby kangaroo!

Special thanks to the photographers and institutions that made ZooBorns! possible:

Cover:
VANCOUVER ISLAND MARMOT
John Ternan/Calgary Zoo

GIANT PANDA
Yun Zi
Zoological Society of San Diego

GENTOO PENGUIN
Bob Couey/SeaWorld San Diego

PYGMY HIPPOPOTAMUS
Prince Harry
Tammy Moult/Cango Wildlife Ranch

EMPEROR TAMARIN
Lucy
Dave Parsons/Denver Zoo

TAWNY FROGMOUTH
Sawyer
Jason Collier/SeaWorld, Orlando

ASIAN SMALL-CLAWED OTTERS
Jason Collier/SeaWorld Orlando

COMMON WOMBAT
Matari
Lorinda Taylor/Taronga Zoo

CROWNED SIFAKA
Tahina
Musée de Besançon

WILDCATS
Joachim S. Muller taken at Opel Zoo

RED KANGAROO
Rooby
Darlene Stack/Assiniboine Park Zoo

Hello, Mommy

ZooBorns!

by Andrew Bleiman and Chris Eastland

The photos in this book were previously published in
ZooBorns: The Newest, Cutest Animals from the World's Zoos and Aquariums.

Ready-to-Read

Simon Spotlight
New York London Toronto Sydney New Delhi

SIMON SPOTLIGHT
An imprint of Simon & Schuster Children's Publishing Division
1230 Avenue of the Americas, New York, New York 10020
Text copyright © 2013 by ZooBorns LLC
Photos copyright © 2010 by ZooBorns LLC
The photos in this book were previously published in *ZooBorns: The Newest, Cutest Animals from the World's Zoos and Aquariums.*
All rights reserved, including the right of reproduction in whole or in part in any form.
SIMON SPOTLIGHT, READY-TO-READ, and colophon are registered trademarks of Simon & Schuster, Inc.
For information about special discounts for bulk purchases, please contact Simon & Schuster Special Sales at 1-866-506-1949 or business@simonandschuster.com.
Manufactured in China 0915 SDI

Welcome to the wonderful world of
ZooBorns!

The newborn animals featured in this book live
in zoos around the world. Get to know them through
adorable photos and fun facts written in language that is
just right for emerging readers. Your child might not be
able to pronounce all the animal species names yet, but if
you stay close by, you can help sound them out.

This book can also be used as a tool to begin a
conversation about endangered species. The more
we learn about animals in zoos, the more we can do
to protect animals in the wild. Please visit your
local accredited zoo or aquarium to learn more!

Baby flamingo is hungry.
Mommy flamingo is there
to give her baby something
to eat.

Hello, mommy flamingo!

Stay close to mommy,
baby zebra!
A baby Grevy's zebra can
run along with the herd
when it is only an hour old.

Hello, mommy zebra!

Hang tight, baby tamandua!
Northern tamanduas
are anteaters.
A grown-up tamandua
can eat 9,000 ants in a day!

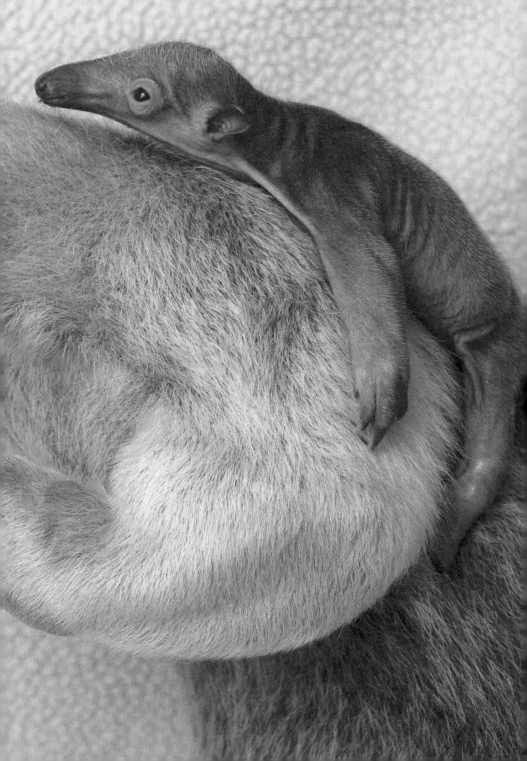

Hello, mommy tamandua!

These furry cuties are
Vancouver Island marmots.
They touch noses to say hi.
Can you touch noses with
someone you love?

Hello, mommy marmot!

This mommy swift fox watches over her babies. Swift foxes are small . . . as small as house cats!

Hello, mommy swift fox!

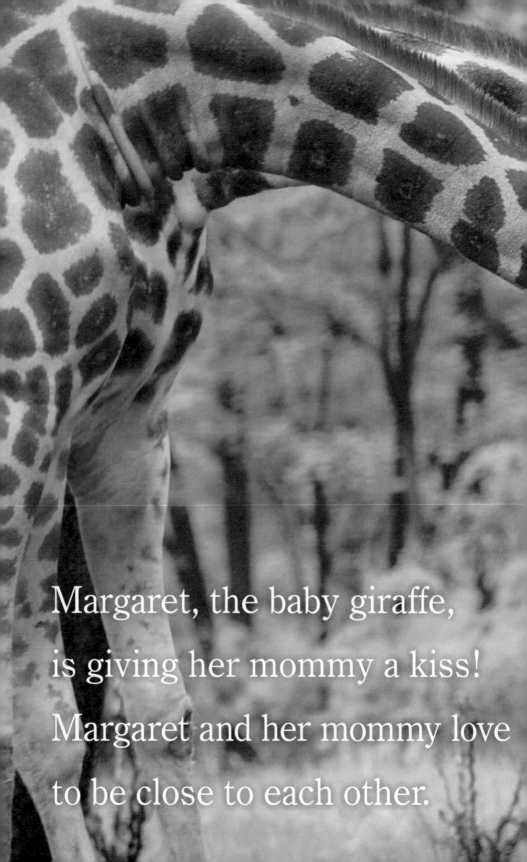

Margaret, the baby giraffe, is giving her mommy a kiss! Margaret and her mommy love to be close to each other.

Hello, mommy giraffe!

This baby white rhinoceros weighed 100 pounds at birth. That is a big baby! Someday she will be as big as her mommy.

Hello, mommy rhinoceros!

This mommy western
lowland gorilla adopted this
baby as her own!

His name is Hasani.

They love to play!

Hello, mommy gorilla!

Miki, the baby beluga whale, swims with his mommy. Beluga whales squeal, chirp, and make lots of other noises when they swim.

Hello, mommy beluga whale!

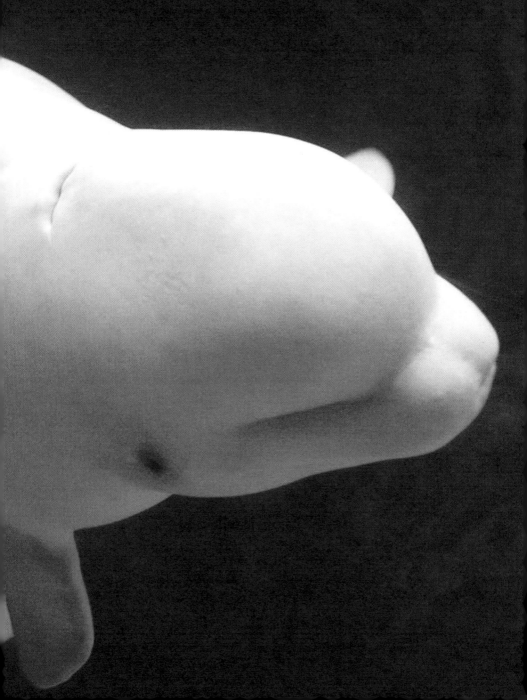

Willie, the mommy chimpanzee, carries her baby wherever she goes. At night, she builds a nest in a tree where they sleep.

Hello, mommy chimpanzee!

Special thanks to the photographers and institutions that made ZooBorns! possible:

AMERICAN FLAMINGO
Ron Brasington/Riverbanks Zoo and Garden

GREVY'S ZEBRA
Matt Marriott/Busch Gardens, Tampa Bay

NORTHERN TAMANDUA
Jason Collier/Discovery Cove

VANCOUVER ISLAND MARMOT
John Ternan/Calgary Zoo

SWIFT FOX
Jennifer Potter/Calgary Zoo

GIRAFFE
Margaret Abigail
Julie Larsen Maher © WCS/WCS's Bronx Zoo

WHITE RHINOCEROS
Matt Marriott/Busch Gardens, Tampa Bay

WESTERN LOWLAND GORILLA
Bawang and Hasani
Marianne Hale/San Francisco Zoo

BELUGA WHALE
Miki
Brenna Hernandez/© Shedd Aquarium

CHIMPANZEE
Willie and Wingu
A.J. Haverkamp/Dierenpark Amersfoort

Nighty Night,

ZooBorns

by Andrew Bleiman and Chris Eastland

Most of the photos in this book were previously published in *ZooBorns: The Newest, Cutest Animals from the World's Zoos and Aquariums*; *ZooBorns Cats!: The Newest, Cutest Kittens and Cubs from the World's Zoos*; and *ZooBorns: The Next Generation: Newer, Cuter, More Exotic Animals from the World's Zoos and Aquariums*.

Ready-to-Read

Simon Spotlight
New York   London   Toronto   Sydney   New Delhi

SIMON SPOTLIGHT

An imprint of Simon & Schuster Children's Publishing Division

1230 Avenue of the Americas, New York, New York 10020

Text copyright © 2013 by ZooBorns LLC

Photos copyright © 2010, 2011, 2012, 2013 by ZooBorns LLC

Most of the photos in this book were previously published in *ZooBorns: The Newest, Cutest Animals from the World's Zoos and Aquariums*; *ZooBorns Cats!: The Newest, Cutest Kittens and Cubs from the World's Zoos*; and *ZooBorns: The Next Generation: Newer, Cuter, More Exotic Animals from the World's Zoos and Aquariums*.

All rights reserved, including the right of reproduction in whole or in part in any form.

SIMON SPOTLIGHT, READY-TO-READ, and colophon are registered trademarks of Simon & Schuster, Inc.

For information about special discounts for bulk purchases, please contact Simon & Schuster Special Sales at 1-866-506-1949 or business@simonandschuster.com.

Manufactured in China 0915 SDI

Welcome to the wonderful world of
ZooBorns!

The newborn animals featured in this book live
in zoos around the world. Get to know them through
adorable photos and fun facts written in language that
is just right for emerging readers. Your child might not
be able to pronounce all the animal species names yet,
but if you stay close by, you can help sound them out.

This book can also be used as a tool to begin a
conversation about endangered species. The more
we learn about animals in zoos, the more we can do
to protect animals in the wild. Please visit your
local accredited zoo or aquarium to learn more!

**Note to readers: Some of the animals in this book are
nocturnal, which means that they are awake at night and
asleep during the day. But that does not mean we cannot
say "nighty night" to them when it is their bedtime.**

Kito is a Hamadryas baboon.
At night, baboons, like Kito,
snuggle with hundreds
of other baboons.

That is a big slumber party!

Nighty night, baby baboon.

Siku, the polar bear cub, loves to play on the ice. At bedtime he loves sleeping on his warm blanket.

Nighty night,
baby polar bear.

These snow leopards
do not need pajamas
to keep warm.
They wrap their tails around
their necks like scarves.

Nighty night, baby snow leopards.

When it is time for bed, this Senegal bushbaby calls out to his friends, and they all cuddle up!

Nighty night,
baby bushbaby.

Red pandas love to eat
bamboo leaves.
Right now these red pandas
are ready for bed.

Nighty night, baby red pandas.

Ruth is a Hoffmann's two-toed sloth.
Sloths move very slowly, especially at bedtime!

Nighty night, baby sloth.

Look at Pepe yawn!
It is time for this maned
wolf pup to hit the hay.

Nighty night,
baby maned wolf.

Pan is not tired at all.

He is an aye-aye.

At night he looks for grubs to eat.

But even Pan has to sleep.

He sleeps during the day!
Nighty night, baby aye-aye.

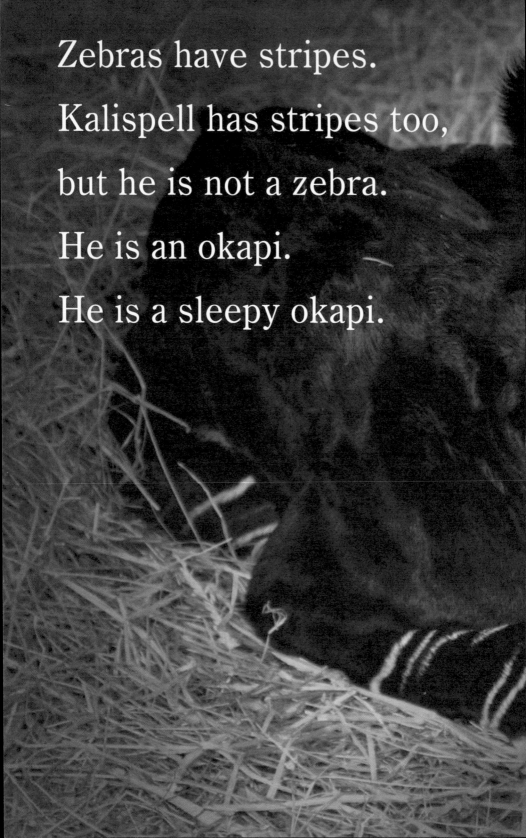

Zebras have stripes.
Kalispell has stripes too,
but he is not a zebra.
He is an okapi.
He is a sleepy okapi.

What will Kalispell
dream about?
Nighty night, baby okapi.

Blitz had a big day!
Now this Eurasian lynx
is tucked in tight
under the covers.
He wants a good-night kiss!

Nighty night, baby lynx.

Special thanks to the photographers and institutions that made ZooBorns! possible:

Cover:
ASIAN SMALL-CLAWED OTTER
Sheri Horiszny/Santa Barbara Zoo

HAMADRYAS BABOON
Kito
Julie Larsen Maher © WCS

HOFFMAN'S TWO-TOED SLOTH
Ruth
Amelia Beamish/Rosamond Gifford Zoo

POLAR BEAR
Siku
© Søren Koch/Hilmer &
Koch Nature Photography

MANED WOLF
Pepe
Tom Svensson/Norden's Ark

SNOW LEOPARD
Kira Victoria and Pasha Ryan
Ken Ardill

AYE-AYE
Pan
Dave Parsons/Denver Zoo

SENEGAL BUSHBABY
Ryan Hawk/Woodland Park Zoo

OKAPI
Kalispell
Dave Parsons/Denver Zoo

RED PANDA
Debbie Ryan/Cotswold Wildlife Park

EURASIAN LYNX
Blitz
Christian Sperka

Splish, Splash,

ZooBorns!

by Andrew Bleiman and Chris Eastland

Most of the photos in this book were previously published in
ZooBorns: The Newest, Cutest Animals from the World's Zoos and Aquariums;
ZooBorns Cats!: The Newest, Cutest Kittens and Cubs from the World's Zoos;
*ZooBorns: The Next Generation: Newer, Cuter, More Exotic Animals from the
World's Zoos and Aquariums*; and *ZooBorns: Motherly Love*.

Ready-to-Read

Simon Spotlight
New York   London   Toronto   Sydney   New Delhi

SIMON SPOTLIGHT

An imprint of Simon & Schuster Children's Publishing Division

1230 Avenue of the Americas, New York, New York 10020

This Simon Spotlight edition June 2015

Most of the photos in this book were previously published in *ZooBorns: The Newest,
Cutest Animals from the World's Zoos and Aquariums*; *ZooBorns Cats!: The Newest, Cutest Kittens
and Cubs from the World's Zoos*; *ZooBorns: The Next Generation: Newer, Cuter, More Exotic Animals
from the World's Zoos and Aquariums*; and *ZooBorns: Motherly Love*.

Text copyright © 2015 by ZooBorns LLC

Photos copyright © 2010, 2011, 2012, 2015 by ZooBorns LLC

For information about special discounts for bulk purchases, please contact Simon & Schuster Special Sales
at 1-866-506-1949 or business@simonandschuster.com.

Manufactured in China 0915 SDI

Welcome to the wonderful world of
ZooBorns!

The newborn animals featured in this book live
in zoos around the world. Get to know them through
adorable photos and fun facts written in language that
is just right for emerging readers. Your child might not
be able to pronounce all the animal species names yet,
but if you stay close by, you can help sound them out.

This book can also be used as a tool to begin a
conversation about endangered species. The more
we learn about animals in zoos, the more we can do
to protect animals in the wild. Please visit your
local accredited zoo or aquarium to learn more!

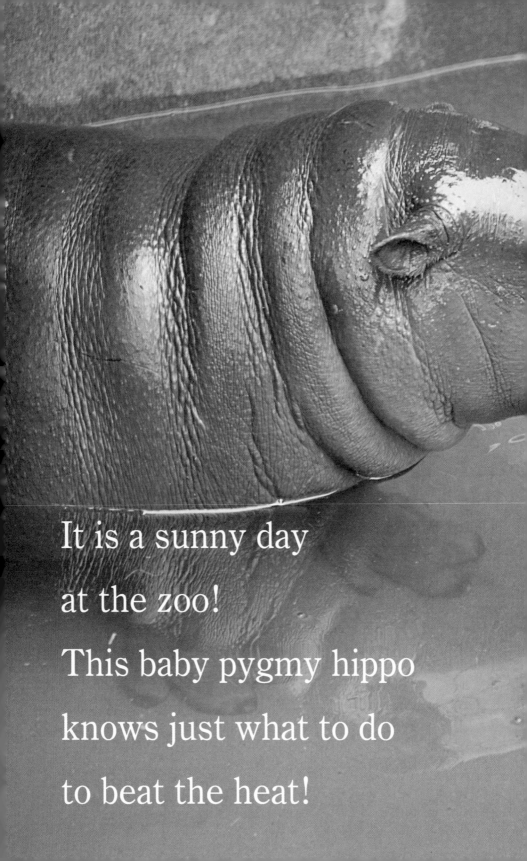

It is a sunny day
at the zoo!
This baby pygmy hippo
knows just what to do
to beat the heat!

Splish, splash,
baby pygmy hippo!

Who loves floating?

Sekiu, a baby sea otter!

To make it easier,

her mommy fluffs her fur

until it is full of air.

Splish, splash,
baby sea otter!

Valentine is a happy
baby American manatee.
He loves warm weather,
he loves the water,
and he loves his mommy!

Splish, splash,
baby American manatee!

It is bath time for Lily,
a baby Asian elephant.
She uses her trunk
to spray water!
It keeps her cool and it is fun!

Splish, splash,
baby Asian elephant!

This baby potbellied pig is taking a mud bath. Pigs love mud puddles. Mud keeps the sun from burning their skin!

Splish, splash,
baby potbellied pig!

Here is a fun fact about baby green sea turtles. In the wild, they hatch and head straight to the ocean!

Splish, splash,
baby green sea turtles!

Swimming is more fun with flippers and whiskers. Just ask a baby sea lion! Whiskers help them find their way in the dark.

Splish, splash,
baby sea lion!

Say hello to Nunavik,
a baby beluga whale.
Beluga whales are called
the canaries of the sea.
They chirp while they swim!

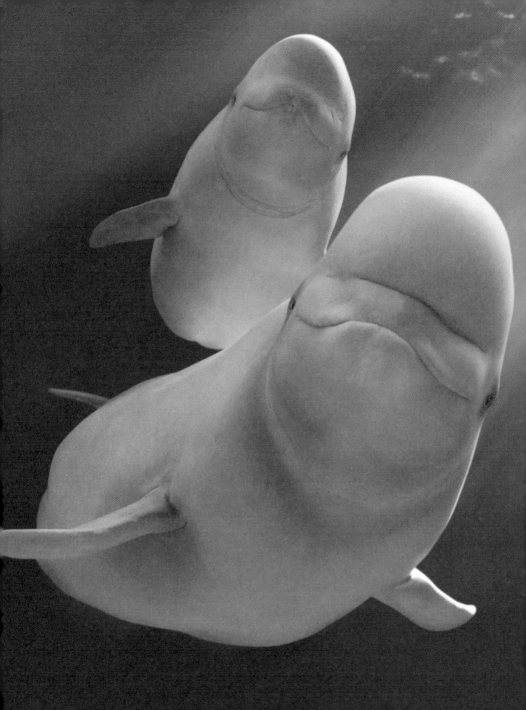

Splish, splash,
baby beluga whale!

These baby fishing cats have webbed toes that help them swim better than most cats. They look ready to dive in!

Splish, splash,
baby fishing cats!

It would be so fun to
play in the waves with this
baby bottlenose dolphin.
Soon he will learn
to do flips!

Splish, splash,
baby bottlenose dolphin!

Special thanks to the photographers and institutions that made ZooBorns! possible:

Cover:
CALIFORNIA SEA LION
Mary Kantarelou/Attica Zoological Park

PYGMY HIPPO
Zola
Dave Parkinson/Tampa's Lowry Park Zoo

SEA OTTER
Sekiu
C.J. Casson/Seattle Aquarium

AMERICAN MANATEE
Valentine
Wildlife Reserves Singapore/Singapore Zoo

ASIAN ELEPHANT
Lily
Michael Durham/Oregon Zoo

POTBELLIED PIG
Tiergarten Delitzsch

GREEN SEA TURTLE
Bob Couey/SeaWorld San Diego

CALIFORNIA SEA LION
PJ
Christopher Morabito/Seneca Park Zoo

BELUGA WHALE
Nunavik
Brenna Hernandez/Shedd Aquarium

FISHING CAT
David Jenike/Cincinnati Zoo and
Botanical Garden

BOTTLENOSE DOLPHIN
Mike Aguilera/SeaWorld San Diego

Snuggle Up,

ZooBorns!

by Andrew Bleiman and Chris Eastland

Most of the photos in this book were previously published in
ZooBorns, ZooBorns: The Next Generation, and *ZooBorns: Motherly Love.*

Ready-to-Read

Simon Spotlight

New York   London   Toronto   Sydney   New Delhi

SIMON SPOTLIGHT

An imprint of Simon & Schuster Children's Publishing Division

1230 Avenue of the Americas, New York, New York 10020

This Simon Spotlight edition September 2015

Most of the photos in this book were previously published in *ZooBorns*,

ZooBorns: The Next Generation, and *ZooBorns: Motherly Love*.

Text copyright © 2015 by ZooBorns LLC

Photos copyright © 2010, 2012, 2015 by ZooBorns LLC

All rights reserved, including the right of reproduction in whole or in part in any form.

SIMON SPOTLIGHT, READY-TO-READ, and colophon are registered trademarks of Simon & Schuster, Inc.

For information about special discounts for bulk purchases, please contact Simon & Schuster Special Sales

at 1-866-506-1949 or business@simonandschuster.com.

Manufactured in China 0915 SDI

Welcome to the wonderful world of
ZooBorns!

The newborn animals featured in this book live
in zoos around the world. Get to know them through
adorable photos and fun facts written in language that
is just right for emerging readers. Your child might not
be able to pronounce all the animal species names yet,
but if you stay close by, you can help sound them out.

This book can also be used as a tool to begin a
conversation about endangered species. The more
we learn about animals in zoos, the more we can do
to protect animals in the wild. Please visit your
local accredited zoo or aquarium to learn more!

This baby koala
is ready for a nap.
Koalas sleep for
eighteen hours a day!

Snuggle up, baby koala!

Polar bears, like Arktos
and his mom,
live in the Arctic.
It is a cold place to live!

Snuggle up, baby polar bear!

These four baby meerkats
are brothers and sisters.
They do everything
together!

Snuggle up, baby meerkats!

Rooby is a baby kangaroo.
She lives in a fluffy,
warm pouch until
she gets bigger.

Snuggle up, baby kangaroo!

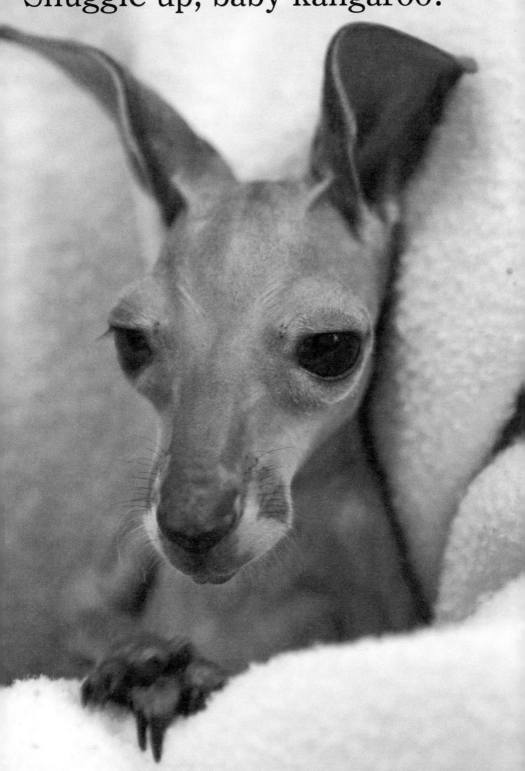

Snow leopards live
high up in the mountains.
Their fur keeps them warm
on chilly days.

Snuggle up, baby snow leopard!

This baby orangutan loves to hug his mom. He holds on to her when she swings from tree to tree.

Snuggle up, baby orangutan!

These baby lions
cuddle with their mom
after a long day
of play.

Snuggle up, baby lions!

The tiny java mousedeer is among the world's smallest hoofed mammals. Fully grown, they weigh less than four pounds.

Snuggle up, baby java
mousedeer!

This flamingo
tucks her baby
under her wing
to keep him safe.

Snuggle up, baby flamingo!

This baby tiger knows that the best thing of all is a hug from his mom.

Snuggle up, baby tiger!

Special thanks to the photographers and institutions that made ZooBorns! possible:

Cover:
KOALA
Richard Rokes/Riverbanks Zoo
and Garden

KOALA
Jonas Verhulst/Planckendael, Taronga Zoo

POLAR BEAR
Arktos
Daniel Zupanc/Zoo Vienna

MEERKATS
Seth Bynam/Point Defiance Zoo
and Aquarium

KANGAROO
Rooby
Darlene Stack/Assiniboine Park Zoo

SNOW LEOPARD
Emmanuel Keller/Zoo Basel

ORANGUTAN
Tatau and Mali
Ray Wiltshire/Paignton Zoo

LIONS
Ryan Hawk/Woodland Park Zoo

JAVA MOUSEDEER
Lumi
Daniel Zupanc/Zurich Zoo

FLAMINGO
Dennis Dow/Woodland Park Zoo

TIGER
Bahagia and CJ
Eric Bowker/Sacramento Zoo